P9-BTY-651

LIFEDREAM

DRAMA SERIES 24

**Canada Council
for the Arts**

**Conseil des Arts
du Canada**

ONTARIO ARTS COUNCIL
CONSEIL DES ARTS DE L'ONTARIO

Guernica Editions Inc. acknowledges the support of The Canada Council for the Arts.
Guernica Editions Inc. acknowledges the support of the Ontario Arts Council.

HERMÉNÉGILDE CHIASSON

LIFEDREAM

A PLAY

TRANSLATED BY JO-ANNE ELDER

GUERNICA

TORONTO · BUFFALO · CHICAGO · LANCASTER (U.K.)

2006

Original title: *La vie est un rêve.*
Copyright © 2006, by Herménégilde Chiasson.
Translation © 2006, Jo-Anne Elder and Guernica Editions Inc.
All rights reserved. The use of any part of this publication, reproduced, transmitted in any
form or by any means, electronic, mechanical, photocopying, recording or otherwise stored
in a retrieval system, without the prior consent of the publisher is an infringement
of the copyright law.

Antonio D'Alfonso, editor
Guernica Editions Inc.
P.O. Box 117, Station P, Toronto (ON), Canada M5S 2S6
2250 Military Road, Tonawanda, N.Y. 14150-6000 U.S.A.

Distributors:
University of Toronto Press Distribution,
5201 Dufferin Street, Toronto (ON), Canada M3H 5T8

Gazelle, White Cross Mills, High Town, Lancaster LA1 1XS U.K.

Independent Publishers Group,
814 N. Franklin Street, Chicago, Il. 60610 U.S.A.

Typeset by Selina.
First edition.
Printed in Canada.

Legal Deposit – First Quarter
National Library of Canada
Library of Congress Catalog Card Number: 2005931735
Library and Archives Canada Cataloguing in Publication
Chiasson, Herménégilde
Lifedream / Herménégilde Chiasson.
(Drama series ; 24)
Translated by Jo-Anne Elder.
Translation of a play originally written in French
under working title:
La vie est un rêve.
ISBN 1-55071-207-1
I. Elder, Jo-Anne II. Title. III. Series.
PS8555.H465L59 2005   C842'.54   C2005-905215-5

LIFEDREAM

I

1
THE LAND IN THE CLOUDS
WHERE DESIRE IS BORN

We were walking through the forest
Heading towards a refuge, a boundary.
Everyone wearing a mantle of light
Everyone holding a glass ball in one hand
And we were seeking the heart of the world.

[All four characters are on stage, but they have no set place to stand, no space other than the inner space of their silent worlds. This is, actually, a dreamspace. Sometimes they look at each other, spy on each other and speak to each other in their inner voices, but they never manage to make real contact with each other. It is as though their speech came from the unconscious rather than conscious thought.]

SOLANGE: I'm dreaming that I'm walking around in a library, a huge library. There are things like cells. On either side of a long hallway. There are lots of them. Inside each one, there are books that I've read. The books on the tables are books that I've read, and the ones on the shelves are books that I haven't read. Each room has its own subject. When I look around at the tables, I get the feeling that I haven't really read much and that there are so many books left to read. I feel ignorant because of all of these books I haven't read. It's as though they're criticizing me.

THOMAS: It's autumn in my dream. It's been raining for days. It's windy, damp and cold. I am in the church I used to go to as a child, and I'm waiting to see God. Waiting for Him to make an appearance. I've been fasting for months so that this great event would finally happen. Somewhere in the room somebody's laughing at the idea that I could actually hope to see God, face to face. Making fun of this desire I have to see Him. But when I turn around, no one's there. And yet . . . Well, I say to myself, I guess it was just the wind.

GABRIELLE: I'm at the hospital. It's my day off but I've been called back in. Something catastrophic has happened. I'm not sure what. People keep coming in on stretchers and you can hear these sirens coming from every direction. The afternoon cries out, the sun cries out, the earth cries out. We don't have enough supplies to treat everybody. I'm the one who has to go and bring the patients up to the operating rooms. Every time I come out to get one, there are more people crying out for help. Every time I leave, my heart breaks because there is all this pain, all this suffering, and there's only so much I can do. I can't give my whole self.

PAUL: Here I am, this guy who never dreams, and I'm dreaming that I'm the one who happens to be in the right place at the right time. When I get to the bank there's money everywhere. Someone forgot to clean it up and there is money all over: bills on the floor, on the counters and even stuck to the ceiling. The janitor is standing there and I ask him what all this means. He tells me that it doesn't mean anything anymore and that he has better things to do.

THOMAS: Someone knocks at the door to tell me that my sister has hanged herself. I don't want to leave the Church because I've been waiting all my life to see the true face of God. I know that He will appear to me that night. I want Him to appear. I want to force Him to show Himself to me.

GABRIELLE: I walk across the waiting room. The floors are covered with blood. The wounded are lying on top of the dead. Their faces are wracked with anger. Their pain is intolerable. There's nothing more I can do for them. That's what I keep telling them. They cling to me, cling to my clothes. I'm afraid they will rip my dress. I'm afraid to see my body naked and covered with blood. Soiled with blood. I'm not like them. I'm not with them. I haven't lived through their tragedy. But they don't hear what I'm saying. They won't let go. They stick to my skin. They're eating me alive. All of a sudden I get the feeling that the library is turning into something else. Something like a prison. Someone has the key of knowledge around his neck. It's a gold key, a little like the golden keys you read about in fairy tales and a voice tells me that this key is the only one to my treasure trove. I feel like I've been caught under a bad spell, and to be freed from it I will have to read all of the books in the library. Unless I meet a man with a pure heart. I'm blinded by the light radiating from the key. It burns my eyes.

THOMAS: I continue to pray. I am kneeling in the middle of the choir loft and light is falling on me as though there is a projector focussed on me. The light is blinding. I can't raise my eyes to heaven because there's so much light. I'm afraid of losing my sight. I can still hear that laugh. It reminds me of my vanity and makes me conscious of the fact that God does not always appear to those who seek Him out. My sister comes through one of the doors. She is naked. Her body is marked, as if she has been scratched. She's walking on the arm of the man who has been laughing. I take off my shirt and tell her to cover up. She just laughs, harder and harder. His laugh is contagious and she has caught it. Suddenly I get frightened. I'm afraid that God won't come if they stay here like this. They've committed a sacrilege against His temple.

PAUL: I'm standing there in the middle of my office. I try to get the regional manager on my cell phone. Or the head office, I'm not sure, but anyway I keep getting the same number. It's a woman's voice, asking if I still love her. But I just want to talk to the damn manager. I keep asking her to put me through; she bursts out laughing. This really vulgar laugh.

SOLANGE: I get the feeling they've built this prison just for me. It is filled with a paralyzing silence. I can go anywhere I want inside the prison. When I walk, I can hear my footsteps echo in my head. The noise is so loud I'm afraid to walk. It hurts my ears. But I have to keep walking to get to the books. I start to read.

GABRIELLE: Every time I go out, the room gets bigger. I'm getting used to seeing them. Now there are injured patients as far as the eye can see. They are still crying out but it's like a hum. I am having an affair with a doctor. Life is shaping up differently now. Death has become a way of life. We have cut the number of operations down to four a day. Outside there are people shooting each other, selling all their belongings, selling their bodies on the street in the hope of living a little longer.

PAUL: I make a date with the woman who was laughing. We are supposed to meet at nine o'clock, but that's the time I have to go back to the bank. I absolutely have to be back in my office then. I am trying to figure out how I'm going to do both.

SOLANGE: The books take longer and longer to read. Each book has its own personality. There are books with little tiny writing. I spend hours staring at them trying to make out the meaning of each sentence. Then there are others with letters running across the page like little ants. And still others with letters that vanish, disappear off the page as soon as I open them.

THOMAS: I hear someone breathing. This time there really is someone. He looks just like the devil I used to see in pictures when I was a child, the one who took the soul of the sinner away with him off to hell. I tell him to get back, that there is no place for him in this church and he tells me that he is everywhere and that he will go and tell God what I really think of Him. I cry out to him to go away. He roars and the walls shake from the thunder of his voice.

GABRIELLE: In the multitude of broken bodies, I see a man I once loved. He is covered with burns. He doesn't say anything. He doesn't even recognize me. No matter how often I say I know him, he won't reply. He just keeps showing me these thousand-dollar bills. He gives me a thousand-dollar bill every time I kiss him. I tell him that it isn't worth anything anymore. He doesn't listen. He knows he is about to die.

SOLANGE: I take out a book and it starts talking to me. Then it is transformed into a man's face. His lips stick out of the paper. I lean over to kiss him but I can't figure out if it is someone I knew or not. Just as I am about to touch his lips, he disappears, and I feel my mouth against this paper that is so rough my lips start bleeding. When I look up again, I see what is written on the page. It is an escape route, a way to get out of prison. I'm supposed to meet the man that very afternoon.

PAUL: It is nine o'clock, and I still don't know what to do. I open the door. The woman is there. She starts to laugh. Even though I keep telling her to be a little more discreet, to be subtle and that I'll see her at lunch time, she just keeps on laughing. She's a complete stranger to me. I can't place her at all. I would love to just push her into my office and grab her, but I'm afraid someone would walk in on us. Afraid she'd laugh even louder. Afraid of not living up to her expectations and making her laugh even harder.

THOMAS: I throw my face onto the ground. Into the dirt. Instead of the little wooden church I went to as a child, I find myself prostrate on the cold stone floor of an old cathedral. I am to be judged for having been willful, for having tried to force God's hand. I am filled with shame. I know I shall be condemned, subjected to the anguish of other people.

GABRIELLE: The man has died in my arms. I am sitting next to him. I beg his forgiveness. Forgiveness for his death. I know very well that my own death is not far off; it is catching up to me. We are all going to die of exhaustion.

There's no one to take our place. They have set fires in the operating rooms, ransacked the medicine cabinets. Those who are still able to walk have taken off to the coast. There are epidemics and horrid diseases. We can't bury the dead anymore. They just lie there, looking at us. With a horrible look in their eyes. Horribly vacant.

SOLANGE: There is no one waiting for me when I get out of prison. Nothing waiting except the oppressive heat and the taste of ashes in my mouth.

PAUL: The employees have arrived. They look at me as though I've just spent the night in the bank with that woman. They seem to be accusing me of opening the safe and throwing the money onto the floor. They put the money in their pockets. She is laughing at them, as she watches me. As though I was her witness.

GABRIELLE: The refugees are walking in single file ahead of us. Now we have caught up to them. Everybody has become resentful because we haven't found a cure. Everyone is trying to survive. Each day passes as slowly as a bad year. I am walking behind my own body. I am following it. My body feels as if it has been emptied by love. Cleaned out. There is no horizon ahead of me.

THOMAS: Suddenly, I hear someone speaking to me in a really soft voice, very faint, telling me to get up. I finally get up the nerve to look around me. I am in a magnificent flower garden. The voice tells me not to be afraid. Not to desire a perfection which is out of my reach. God will not come. He is very busy. He has sent me a message not to wait for Him. To live in the meantime. I can't recognize the face of the person talking to me, only the voice. The voice of a friend that I helped to die. A long time ago.

PAUL: It is ten o'clock; the customers arrive. She goes up to them. Tells them all kinds of things about me, about what we were doing together. Really personal things. She is lying. I want to die. I am ashamed, I want to hide my face for the rest of my life. I go into my office. The phone rings. In real life, as well, the phone is ringing.

SOLANGE: I start screaming. Calling out for someone. Calling out for help. The sound of my own voice has woken me up.

THOMAS: When I wake up, I have the impression, just for a moment, that someone is sitting on my bed. I think I see someone from the back. Someone dissolving into the darkness. It is raining and I can hear thunder.

GABRIELLE: I hear my heart beating like a tidal wave. I'm afraid of drowning. The man sleeping next to me wakes me up because I'm screaming. He's afraid, too. Afraid without knowing why. Afraid of my fear.

2
GOLD AND THE WEIGHT OF LIFE

Day pushed night down the stairs
Life is a calendar filled with promises
Life is a book that we never stop writing.
Life is a cornflake floating in a sea of milk,
a continent drifting away in a china bowl.

SOLANGE: Last night, I had the weirdest dream. We were out walking in a snowstorm, you and I. We had run out of gas. We were trying to find someone who could get us some, but everyone we met was dressed in clothing from another century. They were all speaking a foreign language. When we talked to them, we couldn't convince them that we were in need because they couldn't even figure out what a car was. The more we tried to explain, the more they looked at us as though we were crazy. They looked at each other . . . Lots of people like that . . . They looked down at the ground or up at the sky . . . Strange, eh?

PAUL: It must be something you were reading that got mixed up with something you did during the day.

SOLANGE: You alway find some way of reducing things to the lowest common denominator . . . triviliazing things . . . trivializing the whole world . . .

PAUL: Okay. Okay. I get the point . . .

SOLANGE: It's not my fault that you don't have dreams.

PAUL: That's not true. Everyone dreams, but probably I don't remember mine. Sometimes I think it's just as well.

SOLANGE: Maybe you do everything in your power so you won't remember.

PAUL: I'm the dreamless model.

SOLANGE: Thanks for telling me. So, anyway, we went into this store to buy clothes . . .

PAUL: When was that?

Solange: In my dream.

PAUL: Oh, yeah! Your dream! I'm getting the idea that it's a long dream . . .

SOLANGE: What's that supposed to mean? It's a dream. How many times have I sat here listening to your money things? Pardon me, I mean your financial matters . . .

PAUL: What I do during the day is real. On the other hand, you, at night . . .

SOLANGE: Go on, finish your sentence.

PAUL: Listen, Solange, a dream is a dream. It isn't going to change your life. We're certainly not going to . . .

SOLANGE: If we were to dream a little more, maybe we'd be able to figure out what's happening around us, in these empty spaces. Maybe we'd be able to see over the wall instead of ramming our noses into it every time we move.

PAUL: Your dreams will end up costing us a lot of money.

SOLANGE: Funny you should say that. Because in my dream, once we got into the store, we tried to buy clothes because we wanted to dress like the other people, but our money had no value because they only accepted gold and we only had our credit cards. And when we told them that they were like money, they burst out laughing. They all had rotten teeth. It was disgusting. That's when I woke up. It was three in the morning. I went down to the living room. I started reading. It was snowing. The cat wanted to be let out. I pretended I didn't hear him. I turned on the light. He finally calmed down and we sat there together watching the snow fall outside the patio doors. It was like we were in a film. The rhythm of the snow was hypnotic. I opened the door and the cat disappeared into the white snow. I went back upstairs. It must have been about four.

PAUL: I didn't hear anything.

SOLANGE: I don't know what's happening to me these days, but it's as if the more I sleep, the less rest I get. Maybe I should get more exercise, do something that would really tire me out.

PAUL: Here I go again, explaining things as simple as all the world to financial illiterates. I feel like I'm quoting myself . . .

SOLANGE: And if you didn't do that, you couldn't go on living, because money is the only thing that excites you . . .

PAUL: At least it serves the purpose of waking people up. *[As though quoting the 6/49 ad:]* "Everybody's got a dream." Drive down the road throwing hundred dollar bills out the window, and you'll see how many people would walk on their children's heads to catch one.

SOLANGE: What are you going to talk to them about?

PAUL: Who?

SOLANGE: I don't know, that group you're meeting at noon.

PAUL: You mean the circle of secretarial visionaries?

SOLANGE: Is that what they call themselves?

PAUL: No, of course not. That's just what I call them.

SOLANGE: Well, there certainly are a lot of cults these days. Why not a cult of secretaries who have visions, after all?

PAUL: No, no, this thing is far less intriguing than that. I'm supposed to talk to them about how they can diversify their investments in order to have a more balanced portfolio and to better manage their assets.

SOLANGE: Mmm. Fascinating.

PAUL: What kind of attitude is that? Fascinating. Like I was some kind of a moron.

SOLANGE: Whoa! Hold on a minute! What's with you today? You've hardly touched your food.

PAUL: Always putting sand in the gear box. How would you feel if I said something like that, or if I reacted that way to one of your dreams?

SOLANGE: Yeah, well, you're not exactly brimming over with enthusiasm, either.

PAUL: What do you want from me? You want me to follow you into another century? At least I listen to what you have to say. You can give me that.

SOLANGE: So you've managed to put your grain of sand in there too. I'm the one who always ends up looking like a flake, while you pass yourself off for a well-adjusted gentleman who talks real business . . .

PAUL: That's your interpretation.

SOLANGE: It's my roundabout way of saying what's going on in my head. I thought that we could tell each other our dreams because I find we don't talk very much to each other anymore. Not about anything real.

PAUL: And dreams are real.

SOLANGE: If you know how to listen, you'll see they're a lot more real than most things that happen. But you . . .

PAUL: I don't remember them. I never remember.

SOLANGE: Have you ever thought that it might be a handicap?

PAUL: I do my dreaming during the day. And usually about things that are possible.

SOLANGE: Like what?

PAUL: I don't know. I think about the day we'll be able to build a real home on that country lot we have. Or maybe buy a sailboat and spend two months of the year down south.

SOLANGE: All right, already. I get it.

PAUL: See? Always the same grain of sand. It's as if you think you can predict my whole life, while yours remains a mystery.

SOLANGE: You know what? I feel the same way.

PAUL: What do you mean, the same way?

SOLANGE: Maybe what I'm telling you is too complicated. You're smart enough, but your brain just doesn't seem to have whatever program it takes to access my way of thinking.

PAUL: Obviously, that's where you draw the line between the spiritual and the material. You put me in the category of base, human activity. The material world. A rat, a larva, a pebble. You, on the other hand, float around the face of God. I'm the low-life and you're way up there in the higher spheres of consciousness.

SOLANGE: I only meant that we don't see life the same way. We don't have the same vision.

PAUL: Or the same blind spots. Whose fault is that?

SOLANGE: Right, whose fault? Like it always has to be someone's fault. Someone must be to blame. Because if you can't blame someone, you can't go on living. It's obvious, or else the opposite would have been proven long ago.

3
RUMOURS OF THE CATACLYSM

One day we will be vaccinated against thirst
One day we will take misery in hand
One day we will trade stars for space
We already know that new planets are being
born in the dust, held tight inside the galaxies.

PAUL *[Enters, reading his speech as though someone has just introduced him]:* I should make a small correction; my name is Paul Mallet and not Maillet as I was introduced. But it's such a common error that I'm not offended in the least. I've been called Paul Mollet, Paul Millet and even Paul Mulet. At least the Paul part seems to come out all right! Anyway, I'd like to begin by saying how pleased I am to have been invited as your guest speaker this month, and I'd also like to say that your organization has made a tremendous step by deciding to give its members a chance to hear about so many different areas of interest. Today, I have been asked to focus on market trends and how they impact on investments and particularly on stocks.

    The first piece of advice that I can offer you is to focus on long-term planning. The market changes frequently and considerably; this can, in fact, be very positive. Change is not always for the worse. It's a little like someone who has just broken up with his or her sweetheart. At the time, that person is not going to be very forward-looking.

    Those who believe that everything is getting worse are prophets of doom. That reminds me of a story I heard back home about an old man who thought the world was coming to an end. When it was windy, he'd say: "The world will end in a gust of wind!" When it was cold, he'd say: "The world will end in ice!" When it was sunny: "The world will end in drought." Well, he ended up being ignored by everyone. His predictions fell on empty ears. *[Changing the subject.]* It's one thing to say that the recession is over, but we still have to figure out how to benefit from the new economy. In other words, how to invest wisely. That means not putting all our eggs into one basket. It really isn't much more complicated than that. For instance, my wife and I have decided to invest two percent of our savings in art. Since we don't know anything about art, we asked an expert for advice. He told us to buy one of Michael Snow's works. I had never heard of this guy, but I figured I could trust my advisor's expertise. When the piece came in from Toronto, we looked at it and said that we'd never put that on our wall. Somebody might come to visit and ask us what it was a picture of. So we put it away in a drawer and let it earn money for us. In ten years, or maybe twenty, depending on whether the artist becomes famous, the piece might be worth something. Now, this might seem like a rather unusual investment, and I probably wouldn't recommend it to anyone else. Not anyone starting out, anyway, because it's a very risky investment. That's why we decided to allocate no more than two percent of our total investment to art. This proportion is what is generally advised for investments qualified as high-risk.

These days, money is on everyone's mind. Everyone is thinking about their future. All that talk about a just society and constitutional reform is off the agenda. We've learned there's no justice and we know who's really the boss. But we've had to pay an arm and a leg to learn our lesson, didn't we? When people have to count their pennies, or politicians cut a little too deep, we know where they're coming from. The world no longer belongs to dreamers and visionaries. The good old days are gone. Today, it's economists who are at the helm. Everyone's hurting, but if you have to cut off a leg to save a life, then that's what you do. It's sad to say, but that's the way it is.

4

THE SOUL AND A REFUGE FOR THE BODY

I spoke of life, the only one I could never have
and you gazed out the window, looking for predictable
answers to questions too large for one person to have.
Maybe we should have chosen silence instead.
Courage to speak. Courage to believe in
the power others have to make the wounds heal over.

GABRIELLE: The other day I went back to church. It was the first Mass I'd been to in about twenty years.

THOMAS: And what did you think?

GABRIELLE: I couldn't stick it out till the end.

THOMAS: You're out of practice.

GABRIELLE: It's changed a lot. I don't know why they had to ruin all the prayers. Before, there used to be something magical about them. A mystery.

THOMAS: Maybe that's because you couldn't understand a word they were saying, back then.

GABRIELLE: Thomas . . . I was driving a car. Another weekend fugue. Another trip to try to forget and I saw people going into a church. It was late in the afternoon. The sky was heavy. Purple, black, heavy. Like the world was about to end. I saw a church in the distance, on the peak of a hill, as if someone had made it appear in a ray of sunlight. I stopped. For no particular reason. It was like a vision . . .

THOMAS: The road to Damascus.

GABRIELLE: The what?

THOMAS: The road to Damascus. That's where Paul was knocked off his horse. Where he had his revelation and was called by God.

GABRIELLE: No, I wasn't knocked out of the car into the canal, or maybe everything would have been much clearer.

THOMAS: Sorry, I didn't mean to interrupt.

GABRIELLE: The light seemed to be bright yellow, standing out against the purple sky. When I got closer, I could see that it was a wedding. What struck me the most was that there was a child standing next to the bride, and he looked like he was seriously disabled, mentally. He was holding onto her skirt like it was a life jacket. They were taking photos, and I thought: what a crazy idea to take pictures before the wedding. It must be bad luck.

THOMAS: Is that true?

GABRIELLE: I don't know. Maybe it's the wedding dress thing, but it seems to me that it could be bad luck. Like selling a bear skin before you've got your hands on it.

THOMAS: B-e-a-r or b-a-r-e skin?

GABRIELLE: Anyway, since I had nothing to do and I didn't know where I was going, I followed them into the church. I was amazed at these crazy gestures they were making, these contortions . . .

THOMAS: You've only been here for an hour and you're already insulting me . . .

GABRIELLE: Thomas, it's not an insult. I just meant to say that I couldn't figure out what they were really thinking, that I had no idea what was going on.

THOMAS: You'll have to go to a proper Mass instead of a surrealistic wedding.

GABRIELLE: Good Lord, you know some big words. It's a good thing you are educated; you make up for the rest of us . . . Se-ri-alistic?

THOMAS: Surrealistic. It means a dreamworld. When reality starts to look like a dream.

GABRIELLE: Really? Well, I left before it was over. You know what weddings do to me. They make me cry. And I figured that since I had come in of my own accord I could leave whenever I felt like it. Especially because the priest was going on about marital fidelity and, since that's hardly my favourite subject these days, I thought I'd be better off having a cigarette.

THOMAS: Have you started smoking again?

GABRIELLE: It's my only vice. Everyone needs one. Besides, you shouldn't talk.

THOMAS: I'll pretend I didn't hear that.

GABRIELLE: Don't worry, I've always had a flair for the dramatic. And I haven't finished my calvary. Remember, it was Christ who carried his cross before being crucified.

THOMAS: How is Claire?

GABRIELLE: She's fine. She's ten years old now. It helps, you know, having a child.

THOMAS: Really?

GABRIELLE: Come on, Thomas, I don't need a sermon.

THOMAS: . . .You said you hadn't been to Mass in twenty years. But when Mom died . . .

GABRIELLE: Yeah, but that's different. You have to follow the crowd in that kind of situation, or else you look like a hard-hearted monster. In the first place, I never take communion. Believe me, at Mom's funeral I could have done without the Mass. I would have rather spent more time talking to people who loved her, listening to stories I hadn't heard. I think I learned more about her in three days than I did in the sixteen years I lived in the same house with her.

THOMAS: May the souls of the faithful dead rest in peace.

GABRIELLE: And may the souls of the faithful living get some right away. Peace. I don't understand why both of us, who come from a dysfunctional family . . .

THOMAS: Dysfunctional? Don't you think that's a bit strong?

GABRIELLE: Well, they didn't label them that way when we were growing up. Otherwise, Thomas, we would have fallen into the severely dysfunctional category.

THOMAS: They did the best they could . . .

GABRIELLE: Forgiveness is your job, not mine. If I want to be . . .

THOMAS: Some day you're going to have to put the past behind you. That's why they bury people.

GABRIELLE: Do you have any idea how often I've dreamed about her? Always the same old dream. For the past three years. I'm in a car, but we've just had an accident. I am lying on top of the man who was driving. Completely naked. It's Claire's father, I think, but I can't be sure. There is blood on my skin. I try to resuscitate the man And all of a sudden Mom opens the car door. She's holding some of my clothes in her hand and telling me I've got to get dressed for church. And suddenly I feel dirty, as though I'm imprisoned in my woman's body, in exile. An awful feeling of shame wakes me up. At least once a week I wake up feeling ashamed of myself. I feel like I'm possessed by a demon, that I need some kind of an exorcism to get it out of my body.

THOMAS: Have you tried to get professional help?

GABRIELLE: Well, at least it doesn't cost as much to confess to a priest, but when you don't believe in anything anymore, or in very much, you know . . .

THOMAS: And you've been having this dream since Mom died, is that what you said? Or did you have it before?

GABRIELLE: Before, I used to have it every six months or so, sometimes more often when things weren't going well. And it wasn't as intense. Maybe it's because she isn't around anymore that she looks larger than life in my dreams.

THOMAS: Have you told anybody else about this? Sometimes just talking about it helps, you know. It's like when you go to confession, you feel released afterwards.

GABRIELLE: You're acting like it's some unforgivable sin.

THOMAS: Perhaps, little sister, you're the only one who can forgive yourself.

GABRIELLE: The body has always been something to mortify. You should never talk about it. You had to take it right to the edge of the abyss to prove that it was doomed to fall. Maybe that's how we ended up with the jobs we have. Trying to help people get over to the other side.

THOMAS: I don't think it's that simple. That's like saying that others are in control of our lives. We're freer than you might think.

GABRIELLE: You tell my patients that, when they find out they're terminal. When their eyes look like they've fallen into the back of their heads and they wonder what kind of hell is waiting for them.

THOMAS: What do you think I do?

GABRIELLE: You? Well, I guess you bring them resignation. May the souls of the dead rest in peace, and then you go back to your TV. I have to live with them all day long, watch their bodies deteriorate, watch the skin melt off their bones, and the only way I can get through it is to get them to rebel, just a little. To have some fun, to know what pleasure is, before they leave. Otherwise, what is the point in having a body? That's why I've always felt dirty, because I've wanted my body to belong to me and to no one else but me. So I could do exactly what I wanted with it . . .

THOMAS: You know I can't think that way . . .

GABRIELLE: No, and neither could she. She didn't want to, either. You have no idea, the kind of things she told me. She never raised her voice; she was always tasteful. Always perfect, but good Lord how she hurt me! I fainted, I held my breath and turned blue inside. I felt like all my strength was dissolving into the ground under my feet. I felt like I had lost the strength of my love, lost it in her pain, in her fear, in her need to be proper, to be perfect, to be immaculate. And I felt so dirty. As if I had betrayed her purity. Betrayed her lily white soul.

5
HUNGER AND ERODING DESIRE

Sit down, and watch the emptiness all around
Even the walls have turned their backs on us
Even the trees will forget our secrets
I don't remember where or when you lost your voice
It is as if I have unlearned the way to speak

PAUL [*Sitting at the table, alone, reading the restaurant menu, when suddenly his cellular phone begins to ring. He takes the call*]: Hello? Yes . . . Yes, I know, but I'm in a restaurant. I guess I can never really escape. There's no place to hide . . . No, no, I forgot to unplug my cellular . . . No, it's all right . . . Whatever you like. I'll be late getting home . . . So how are you doing? Still overworked and underpaid? Yes, but remember, it's spring, and after the spring, there will be the summer holidays, and after the holidays, it's fall again, and after fall, winter . . . I don't think we can do much about it . . . [*Gabrielle enters and sits down.*] I've got to go, the waitress just came to take our order, and since they're pretty slow here, I'd better hurry up. No, no, of course she won't be insulted. They know me, here . . . Right. See you later.
GABRIELLE: Your wife?
PAUL: Yes.
GABRIELLE: She must suspect that something's going on.
PAUL: Why would she suspect?
GABRIELLE: Because she's an intelligent person.
PAUL: You've never even met her.
GABRIELLE: I've designed my own personal police sketch.
PAUL: Based on what information?

GABRIELLE: An angel of the Lord appeared to me one night, just out of the blue, and showed me a portrait of a woman in tears, and when I got closer, I noticed that he was holding up a mirror and I saw my own reflection.

PAUL: Not you, too!

GABRIELLE: What do you mean, me too?

PAUL: What's with all these people thinking their dreams are some kind of sign?

GABRIELLE: Who are you talking about now?

PAUL: Oh, it's just because Solange has got this idea that I should try to remember my dreams.

GABRIELLE: At any rate, I'm not talking about a dream, it's just something I invented. Pure imagination. I was just pretending it was a real dream.

PAUL: What does Solange look like?

GABRIELLE: She's rather tall. Quite pretty, not exactly beautiful, but pretty. Blue eyes, a rather large mouth, blond hair. It's hard to say; when I close my eyes, I can see her, but it's hard to say what I see. Hard to describe.

PAUL: Are you ready to order? I don't see any waiters around.

GABRIELLE: I am the servant of the Lord. I shall serve.

PAUL: Quit fooling around. I will be the Lord's servant, because I'm going to have to go up to the bar to get something to eat.

GABRIELLE: What a dive! It's worse than a bar. A tavern.

PAUL: What do you expect? There aren't many places we can go to hide out. If we go to any of those places you'd prefer, someone is bound to recognize me. Well, I'm off to the bar.

GABRIELLE: [While he is gone, she picks up the cell phone he has left on the table. She pretends to dial.] Hello? Dr. Henry, please . . . Yes, I'm one of his patients . . . Yes, it's an emergency . . . Hi, it's me . . . Yeah, I know you're at the hospital . . . So? She can wait . . . I just wanted to know what you were doing tonight, very late tonight, actually . . . I was hoping we could sleep together, dream together, go off on a trip, take off somewhere together . . . It's no big deal; your patient can wait. I do a lot of waiting myself. What do you mean you're busy tonight? *[Paul returns to the table.]* I have to go now, but I'll see you this afternoon. For sure. Excuse me, I have to go . . . Right, I'll call you back later on.

PAUL *[Sits down]*: So. You know how a cell phone works, do you?

GABRIELLE: I thought this meal was going to be special. So what's happened to it?

PAUL: They'll let me know when it's ready, but I should warn you: they're not known for their speed.

GABRIELLE: I'm used to that kind of service, Paul . . . Anyway, I didn't call you up for a gourmet feast.

PAUL: No, I know, it's to plan that bank robbery we've been talking about so we can take off for Bermuda, right?

GABRIELLE: Better yet: I want us to take off in separate directions.

PAUL: What are you talking about?

GABRIELLE: I've met someone. At any rate, we always knew this was how it would end.

PAUL: Who is he?

GABRIELLE: What does it matter? . . . That's weird. All of a sudden, I feel like I'm having some kind of déjà vu. I get the feeling I've had this same conversation with somebody else.

PAUL: You probably have.

GABRIELLE: I knew you'd hold it against me. As soon as a woman admits she likes sleeping with men, they see her as a sex object.

PAUL: I should have known.

GABRIELLE: Known what? You have a wife to go home to, Paul, but I just go home to my own loneliness. I've only got myself to put my arms around.

PAUL: You're just doing this to try to force me into . . .

GABRIELLE: No, no, no, Paul. This somebody else, he's a real person. I'm not trying any emotional blackmail here. Really. I guess there's nothing I can say to . . .

PAUL: You're doing just fine.

GABRIELLE: I feel like I've messed up, that I've spoiled something . . .

PAUL: Is he someone I know?

GABRIELLE: How could he be someone you know, when we're always hiding out? It would be pretty hard to meet someone where we go. I'm not very good at playing the nagging, possessive mistress.

PAUL: Is he good to you?

GABRIELLE: Yeah, there are still some good ones out there.

PAUL: Anyway, it won't last. They never do, with you.

GABRIELLE: Yes, I'm an angel who crosses people's lives and raises their hearts to her lips. Then I put them back in their chests and fly off again, while they're still lying there with their hard-ons pointed at the sky.

PAUL: Is this another one of your dreams?

GABRIELLE: No, that's reality. Unfortunately. The trouble with my men is that my body, my ass, actually, always hides my heart from them.

PAUL: And this time, the opposite has happened?

GABRIELLE: This time, we have an agreement. In the sense that the man who is . . . Actually, I'm the one who's in love with him. But this man can't make it, at least not with me. So the scenario is very different. I figure there must be something else I love . . .

PAUL: You've always had a weakness for gays.

GABRIELLE: Well, up until now, they've been the only men . . .

PAUL: Some role model.

GABRIELLE: Listen, we have to change the rules of the game.

PAUL: What game?

GABRIELLE: The game of love. The game men and women play.

PAUL: Once we conceive babies in incubators, the rules will change.

GABRIELLE: Since when do you have something against gay men?

PAUL: They're all right as long as I don't find any playing in my back yard.

GABRIELLE: Playing. You see? It is a game.

PAUL: I just wish I hadn't got caught . . .

GABRIELLE: It isn't so bad. You had thirty some-odd years before I came into your life . . .

PAUL: So what? What difference does that make?

GABRIELLE: You're taking it all wrong.

PAUL: Anyway, we're adults. We're reasonable people. We should be able to get over this like a cold, or a case of the flu . . .

GABRIELLE: I'd like to keep on seeing you. I'd like us to be able to talk to each other.

PAUL: Tell me: have you given him your old "I'd like us to take off somewhere together?" It's your best line, your best sales pitch. Don't ever forget that one . . .

GABRIELLE: I hope we'll have something left besides sarcasm once you've got your pride out of the way . . .

PAUL *[Someone is waving to him from the counter.]*: Our order is up. *[He stands up.]* I'll think about it.

6
FLESH AND CROSSING THE DESERT

How do I close the door when you are the home I am fleeing? Your body is an enigma, your face tells me over and over again of your journey; you went to drink from the well of evil. I left you my doubt and you placed it between the pages of a book; then you closed it, and it shall ever remain closed.

[Thomas is sitting reading a book. Suddenly, Solange appears. She has an umbrella and is wearing a wet raincoat. She is holding a black towel. She is dressed completely in red; he, in black. She looks like a devil coming to tempt him. Thunder can be heard during the entire scene.]

THOMAS: Come on in, please.

SOLANGE: Sorry to keep you waiting.

THOMAS: No problem, I was busy reading. *[He shows her the cover of the book, Grand et Petit Albert.]* Listen to this: "To make a girl or a woman admit everything she has done, take the heart of a pigeon and the head of a frog; after drying them out, crush them into powder on the stomach of the female as she sleeps, and she will confess everything that burdens her soul."

SOLANGE: My watch has stopped.

THOMAS: It's three o'clock.

SOLANGE: Half an hour late . . .

THOMAS: Actually, I had given up waiting for you. These storms bother me. There's been thunder every day for two weeks. I always pay attention to the weather; it's an old habit. An obsession, almost.

SOLANGE: Are you superstitious?

31

THOMAS: Oh, good heavens, no! Although I do find that certain things sometimes happen that seem . . . strange. Uncanny. The other day a woman came in here. Someone I had never met. Sometimes people from other parishes come here so they won't be recognized. She had a child with epilepsy that she claimed was possessed by a demon. The child seemed fine to me but she insisted that I do a laying on of hands. To chase out the devil, she said. I told her I wasn't a healer. The woman wasn't young. Then, all of a sudden, she grabbed my hands and put them on top of the child's head and she started screaming: "Deliver us from evil! Deliver us from evil." I must admit, I had trouble getting to sleep that night.

SOLANGE: Don't worry, I didn't come here for anything like that.

THOMAS: I hope not. Otherwise I might start believing that I'm some kind of a saint.

SOLANGE: Someone told me you were interested in Acadian history and I thought you might be able to clarify certain obscure points that have been bothering me, regarding some work I've been asked to do.

THOMAS: Are you Acadian?

SOLANGE: My parents were. So I am, genetically.

THOMAS: My research is just a hobby, you might say, so I haven't done the kind of overview that men of letters . . .

SOLANGE: And women of letters?

THOMAS: Of course. At any rate, I'm always happy to help out historians, if I can answer any of your questions. *[While he is talking, she takes a dictaphone out of her bag, places it on the table, plugs it in and is now taking out a notepad.]*

SOLANGE: You don't mind if I tape this, do you?

THOMAS: As long as it isn't used against me!

SOLANGE: I find it a more faithful record than the written word. *[Checking the dictaphone.]* Hold on . . . There we are. I read somewhere, and I think it is now generally believed, that the Acadian people, at the time of the

Expulsion, sang psalms while they were put aboard the ships.

THOMAS: The Acadians were a very religious people. Without their unshakeable trust in Providence, they would never have managed to endure all the suffering that heaven sent to try them. They were a very peaceful group of people. But, as it is suggested in the Book of Job, God tests the faith of just men as a standard for us all . . .

SOLANGE: Do you have documents that recount these events?

THOMAS: We know they sang hymns. It's written down; I think it's in Winslow's papers. The psalms that were well-known among the Acadians in those days: there weren't very many of them, actually . . .

SOLANGE: Yes. I know there is a reference to one entitled "All things shall pass."

THOMAS: The words to that one are incredible, aren't they? "Under the firmament, all is ever changing, and just as on ice everything is falling, all things shall pass." What a lesson in humility for so many who were headed for death . . .

SOLANGE: Precisely. Don't you have a bit of trouble accepting this idea of a nation of sheep following their destiny that the church has put forward since the time . . .

THOMAS: Listen, Miss, I became interested in Acadian history because of this little incident. The fact that even in such great misfortune, they showed invincible courage. Perhaps this version of history doesn't jive with your rationalist vision or with all of those books you've read. Miss — or is it Madam? . . . [She gestures that it doesn't matter.] . . . Do you have faith?

SOLANGE: How do you define "faith"?

THOMAS: You sound just like Pilate, asking Jesus "What is truth?" Faith is a gift given to us through baptism.

SOLANGE: And what is its purpose?

THOMAS: Belief in God.

SOLANGE: And who is God?

THOMAS: Can't you remember any of your catechism?

SOLANGE: When I was learning it, God was a threat. Then He became a doubt, and now He is pure abstraction. But I get the feeling that He is no longer being held responsible for all the misery we see around us.

THOMAS: Since more than two hundred years ago, since 1755 to be exact, men have decided to reason rather than to believe . . .

SOLANGE: Women too . . .

THOMAS: Yes, but they started a little later. 1755 was the year of the Lisbon earthquake that killed thirty thousand people, and the year that Voltaire launched his venomous attack on the Church. That is when we started turning to science for our answers. Faith has lost a lot of ground since then, and the Church, as well . . .

SOLANGE: You place an awful lot of importance on one man. It has been proven that . . .

THOMAS: You can believe any proof you want to, but the universe has an order that must have been created, must have been willed . . .

SOLANGE: It always comes down to that, doesn't it?

THOMAS: I am afraid that we are treading on dangerous terrain. Would you have a glass of apple juice, orange juice, a Pepsi, maybe? A simple glass of water?

SOLANGE: You want to throw water on the flames?

THOMAS: I'd offer you coffee, but I never drink the stuff.

SOLANGE: Too bad. That's all I drink at this time of night . . . I mean day. What a slip! It helps me get finished.

THOMAS: Coffee is a drug; it ends up taking over the body, and despite all the tests that have proven or disproven it, I'm convinced that sooner or later they'll find out it has a harmful effect on the cardiac system.

SOLANGE: For me, it's like an electric shock that wakes up my thoughts. It gives me the impression that I'm really alive, that I'm in control again . . .

THOMAS: Is that all you wanted to know? Is your machine still on?

SOLANGE: You're right, we got a bit off track. What were we talking about?

THOMAS: The psalms they were singing . . .

SOLANGE: Right, the psalms. What do they represent, according to the Christian tradition?

THOMAS: They are songs of praise to our Creator.

SOLANGE: Yes, but isn't the Song of Songs, which is a book of the Bible, supposed to be a psalm? And it speaks openly about sexual pleasure . . .

THOMAS: That's right. There are exceptions.

SOLANGE: When we were in the convent, they warned us not to spend much time on those pages. In fact, it was against the rules. Naturally, we made sure we found out why as soon as we could. Even memorized long passages of it. At the time, we didn't realize what a beautiful piece it was, what a beautiful poem.

THOMAS: I must admit that I've only read it once.

SOLANGE: I sleep, but my heart waketh:
it is the voice of my beloved
that knocketh, saying,
Open to me, my sister, my love,
my dove, my undefiled; . . .ummmh . . .
for my head is filled with dew,
and my locks with the drops of the night . . . ummmh . . .
I have put off my coat;
how shall I put it on? . . .

THOMAS: You enjoy controversy, don't you?

SOLANGE: I don't know what you mean . . .

THOMAS: You came here to ask questions about history, and instead you want to contest the Church and its doctrines. God is merciful.

SOLANGE: You're certain of that?

THOMAS: It's not up to me to look for certainties. All I have to do is to submit to the plans He has made for me and for all of His creatures.

SOLANGE: I wish I could be that resigned to my fate. I think my life would be simpler.

THOMAS: What you call resignation, I call faith. And you have it too, through your baptism. But the soul is faced with many temptations on the road to salvation . . .

SOLANGE: You believe in evil, is that it?

THOMAS: For a long time I believed that evil was the enemy of good, but now I'm — let's just say that the devil, Satan if you will, is a very peculiar character. Take this woman who came to me with the child she claimed was possessed.

SOLANGE: It's easy to blame Satan. Satan is a victim, when you come right down to it, and evil has a much deeper source.

THOMAS: Evil is when the body forgets the soul.

SOLANGE: What is the soul?

THOMAS: What is truth?

SOLANGE: Lucifer was the most cherished angel in heaven.

THOMAS: And God so loved the world that He gave His only begotten Son . . .

SOLANGE: Oh my! We're having a battle of quotations, are we? *[Turning off her machine.]* I think I'm going to turn off the machine because we are definitely not finding out anything this way. *[They laugh.]*

7

ON THE FINE ART OF DISDAIN

I no longer know your name. I do not pretend anything. You will no longer come to see me. You will forget my address and I'll pretend that I have forgotten your voice. I left something in your soul but I lost the way of my return and your face is nothing but a memory that surfaces when I drown, thinking of your body when I tremble with all my strength.

GABRIELLE: Paul! You're certainly the last person I expected to find here. Usually you don't mix with this crowd.

PAUL: I see you've brought your new . . .

GABRIELLE: I see you've brought your wife. And he isn't my new man. He's someone I care about. This is the perfect time to introduce me to Solange . . .

PAUL: I hope you're not thinking of doing anything foolish. If you do anything that embarrasses me, Gabrielle, you'll regret it more than you've ever regretted anything in your life.

GABRIELLE: I'll do as I please. Who do you think you are?

PAUL: Someone you care about. That's what you told me the other day, right?

GABRIELLE: That was two weeks ago. By the way, I'd like you to stop harassing me at work, or even worse, in the middle of the night.

PAUL: I do what I can to get by.

GABRIELLE: Well, I end up lying awake at nights because of it, if you want to know the truth.

PAUL: So I'm a harasser now, eh? That's not what you thought of me a while back . . .

GABRIELLE: Listen, I don't think this is the place to start up about these things . . .

PAUL: Then let's make a date to discuss them somewhere else. How about tomorrow at noon? That works out well for me; I haven't got anything planned.

GABRIELLE: Can't you understand, Paul, that it's over? It's history now.

PAUL: Maybe for you.

Gabrielle: It's always like that. It's over for one person before it is for the other.

PAUL: I can tell you're speaking from experience.

GABRIELLE: Let's change the subject. Your wife is headed this way.

PAUL: Then go see your . . .

GABRIELLE: No. I want to meet her. All this time . . .

PAUL: Yeah, I really like that little print. A print? That's what it is, isn't it?

GABRIELLE: No, it's a photograph. *[Speaking to Solange.]*

SOLANGE: Did you see something you liked?

PAUL: Yeah, number *[looking in the catalogue]* twenty-one. It's called *Riding on the Wave.*

SOLANGE: With a title like that, you can't go wrong.

PAUL: It isn't very expensive for a big piece like that. A hundred and fifty dollars. It's the piece I like the best. See it, over there? The one next to the red, white and blue scribbles. I met a guy who teaches art history a while ago and he told me that it was a good deal. Apparently he's a young artist with a lot of potential. It's worth it even just as an investment. A hundred and fifty dollars. That's next to nothing. What can you get today for . . .

SOLANGE: Anyway, buy something you'll be able to hang on the wall.

PAUL: You saw it; you know the one I mean.

SOLANGE: Oh, yeah. For me it's six of one and a half dozen of the other. They're all the same. I'd rather have a Rembrandt print . . .

GABRIELLE: Excuse me, I have to be off. See you later, Paul.

SOLANGE: Who's that?

PAUL: Oh, I'm sorry, I forgot to introduce you. I'm so preoccupied by that painting. I was just thinking that I'd better move quickly, because at a hundred and fifty bucks it'll go like that . . . [Snapping his finger.] She's someone I met the other day when I gave that talk to the circle of secretaries.

SOLANGE: At any rate, you two seemed to be involved in some deep discussion.

PAUL: We were talking about modern art. People get excited about modern art . . .

SOLANGE: I didn't know you were interested in modern art, at least not enough to keep up your end of a serious conversation about it . . .

PAUL: From a financial perspective, art can give you good returns on your investment, if you know what you're doing.

SOLANGE: Anyway, make up your mind fast, because I'm getting one of my migraines . . .

PAUL: All right, I'll go ask the guy to put it away for me until tomorrow.

SOLANGE: I'm going to lie down in the car. Don't be long. I really don't want to hang around here much longer.

PAUL: Here, take the keys.

SOLANGE: What for? I'm not going anywhere.

PAUL: You can start the car if you get cold.

SOLANGE: You mean warm it up for you before you get there.

PAUL: Okay, you're right. Go ahead, I'll be right out. [Solange leaves. Paul heads towards the counter. Gabrielle stands in his way.]

GABRIELLE: I just wanted to say that I really appreciated your attitude. Is that what you call a friendly relationship?

PAUL: I seriously wonder if we can be friends after everything that has happened. Especially the way it ended.

GABRIELLE: It ended the way it began, Paul. It was never really love between us. You needed something, I needed something, and that's what we got. It was just screwing

39

and it was good. It did us both a lot of good. Now it's over. That's it.

PAUL: Not here, all right?

GABRIELLE: I didn't start this discussion.

PAUL: I know you don't have a problem with any of this. You need someone? That one there. Why him rather than someone else? They're all the same.

GABRIELLE: You're talking about yourself, not me.

PAUL *[Referring to Gabrielle's man]:* What is so extraordinary about this man, in your opinion? Except that he dresses well and has a made-to-measure face?

GABRIELLE: That's what you see from a distance. When you get close to people, you see them more clearly, Paul. Their whole world rises to the surface . . .

PAUL: Fine, let's go. I want to get up close. Maybe I can fall under his spell too.

GABRIELLE: Paul? Where are you going?

PAUL: I'm going to see him. I have to go right up to him, seeing as I don't know his name. I want to reassure him, because he might get worried if he sees you talking so long with a man he doesn't know. I'm going to introduce myself.

GABRIELLE: Paul, if you do something that stupid I will never speak to you again in your bloody life.

PAUL: All right, then, I want us to get together. Soon. Monday, for lunch. No later.

GABRIELLE: Look how you treated me when Solange arrived. I was nothing. I didn't exist. You could have put your hand through me and felt nothing but air. That's how you acted.

PAUL: I was taken a little aback. If you had waited, I could have figured out how to behave. I think Solange suspects something. And I've got to get out there right away because I get the feeling she could come back any minute.

GABRIELLE: I don't see how she could suspect anything. In a split second I became one of the paintings on the wall. You're so good at that.

Paul: Oh! That reminds me, I have to buy that painting.

Gabrielle: Number 21?

Paul: Yes.

Gabrielle: It's already been sold.

Paul: Sold?

Gabrielle: My nephew is one of the six artists in the exhibition. I decided I should encourage him. He's the one who told me to buy that one. Apparently it's his best work. The title bothers me a bit, *Riding on the Wave,* but I think it's because he's taken with that idea, too, and it must come out in his painting . . .

Paul: So it runs in the family. You should sell it to me if you don't think anymore of it than that.

Gabrielle: Okay. One thousand dollars.

PAUL: Are you crazy?

GABRIELLE: An investment, Paul. I'm a quick study.

PAUL: Yes, but to go from one hundred and fifty to a thousand in ten minutes . . .

GABRIELLE: You're the third person who's asked me to sell it. The rarer the offer and the higher the demand, the more the price increases. You know all about it, don't you, because you're number one in the profit department. You know how to take advantage better than anyone else I know.

PAUL: Stop this foolishness, Gabrielle.

GABRIELLE: That's what your life is like, Paul. You know what makes you act this way.

PAUL: Anyway, this is no place to discuss it. I've got to go. Monday then?

GABRIELLE: What is this business about taking without asking? I'm not an investment, you can't just decide to take me.

PAUL: I'll call you at the hospital. Say hello to your . . . Tell him I'm some great undiscovered artist. He'll understand.

GABRIELLE: Understand what?

PAUL: Why you were talking to me all this time.

8

THE LESSON OF SUFFERING

Every tremor of my heart
Is an earthquake that shakes my body
And life is a series of cataclysms repeating themselves
Until my breath has been taken away by rage and hope
If it weren't for this I would dissolve into tears
If it weren't for this I would burst into pain.

[Gabrielle enters carrying a bag, like a rather small brief-case, and takes out various diagrams and illustrations as she speaks to her audience, during the introductions. Her audience is made up of eight to ten year olds. She address-es them.]

GABRIELLE: Hello. There are more of you today than last week. Congratulations. You're good kids to get up early on a Saturday morning . . . Or maybe we should be con-gratulating your parents because they're the ones who had to get up to drive you here. How are you doing, girls? You seem to be more lively than the boys. You must go to bed earlier.

Today, we're going to be talking about the most important organ or part of the human body. Who knows what that might be? If this organ stops working for three minutes, it's fatal. It's the . . . the heart. Right. So, as we were saying *[she takes out a poster to illustrate the heart]*, when the heart stops beating for three minutes, approxi-mately three minutes, it stops pumping blood to the brain and they figure that it only takes about three minutes for the brain cells to die. The other organs take longer to feel the effects. For example, the liver can take up to three hours to shut down.

So the heart is really a pump that pushes the blood all around the body, a little like a tap, but a tap that turns on and off between seventy and one hundred and twenty times a minute. If you put your finger at the base of your thumb, you can feel the blood surging every time your heart beats. That's what is called the . . . Who knows what it's called? We talked about it at the very beginning . . . It's the . . .? The pulse. Oh! You're still asleep this morning, I guess. I'm sure you really knew it; maybe you were afraid to speak up. So if you squeeze the base of your thumb a bit, you'll feel a kind of tingling under your fingers. That's the blood that comes from the heart and goes all around your body, even in the tiniest little veins. In a way it's like your life is rushing through you when you aren't really paying attention to it, because your heart is a very quiet muscle that you don't notice most of the time.

The heart never stops beating. Unlike other muscles that get tired and need a rest, the heart goes on pumping all day and all night, even when you're dreaming and the rest of your body is having a nap. The heart keeps on working all the time. We might say that the heart is the engine of life.

The heart is also the most popular muscle in the human body. Who can tell me what feeling the heart is associated with . . .? With . . . ? With love. Right! That's why on Valentine's Day we send heart-shaped cards saying how much we care about each other. Because the heart is like love. It is what keeps us alive . . . It's hard to understand, but for now we'll just say that love is something that makes the heart excited, that makes it beat harder and faster, and gives it flight. In other words, the heart is the muscle that keeps us alive, but it is also the part of our body that tells us if we're happy or sad.

Sometimes it happens, though, that the heart wears out. When that happens to someone we call that person a cardiac patient. Car-di-ac. We say that a person has had a cardiac arrest or a heart attack. A heart attack can happen to someone who is feeling just fine, or to someone who is not feeling well. What do we do when it happens? Well, as we were saying a few minutes ago, the brain stops working after just three minutes if the heart isn't nourishing it with blood. So we have to act very quickly.

Intermission

II

9
DESPAIR AS A WAY OF LIFE

I was walking around inhabited by all the world's
   distractions
And I stopped to listen to your confusion
Your voice full of reproach, your heart in tears
You were looking for the place where words are
   lord and master
And I was searching for the secret of all suffering.

[Outside, in a park. We can hear traffic noises, children playing . . .]

SOLANGE: That's right, it's about Paul.

GABRIELLE: How did you find out?

SOLANGE: Because I saw you two at the exhibition the other day. Your discussion was a little heated, I thought. I got the feeling it was more than small talk.

GABRIELLE: If you knew who I was, why did you come over? Weren't you angry?

SOLANGE: Angry? What good would that do? Tell me: what would be the point?

GABRIELLE: When someone cheats on me, I can't even sleep at night. I'm beside myself.

SOLANGE: Did you ever get the feeling that . . .

GABRIELLE: Please, move over closer. There shouldn't be this distance.

SOLANGE *[Slides over closer]*: There. Did you ever get the feeling that men had taken over our lives, to the point that we had given everything up? Given everything to them? Even our children. They have their names, as if they belonged to them. We have their names. It's supposed to be a sign of their love. A sign. Love.

GABRIELLE: They're not all like that.

SOLANGE: Well, it's true for the male we're talking about and that we share . . .

GABRIELLE: Used to share.

SOLANGE: What?

GABRIELLE: That we used to share.

SOLANGE: So you're no longer interested in him?

GABRIELLE: In any case, we were never in love. There was never any question of him leaving you. It was just about . . .

SOLANGE: Sex.

GABRIELLE: I don't know why you should pass judgement on me.

SOLANGE: These things happen, right?

GABRIELLE: I've never met anyone who reacted this way. You're so . . . detached.

SOLANGE: I have learned to work through my life, rather than live it. To be reasonable.

GABRIELLE: Everything important happens in the heart.

SOLANGE: Or, in the case of you and Paul, in the body.

GABRIELLE: Well, it's not quite that simple.

SOLANGE: Anyway, I act with my head and not with my body. As soon as Paul figured that out, he started looking elsewhere. For me, the body is meaningless, a burden, something that gets worn out and that you have to feed, wash, satisfy.

GABRIELLE: My mother looked at life that way, too.

SOLANGE: So you blame her for taking your body away from you. This is how you get your revenge . . .

GABRIELLE: I just told you that what is important to me happens in the heart . . .

SOLANGE: And yet your affair with Paul proves the opposite.

GABRIELLE: We can search all our lives and never find the one thing that matters.

SOLANGE: You wanted to meet Paul's wife, to see what she was like, am I right?

46

GABRIELLE: Everyone needs a body. It is your body that cries, that hurts, that remembers. That is alive. You have to live right to the limits of your body. Once your body is gone, what's left of your life?

SOLANGE: What's left is what you've done with your life.

GABRIELLE: Like what, for instance?

SOLANGE: Like books. Bridges. Roads. Children — the things that are passed on genetically. The consciousness that is passed on from one generation to the next. That's what life is all about. Increasing consciousness. Becoming more aware. Otherwise you fall into the trap of everyday existence. Everything is levelled off, flat. The body takes control . . . Who left?

GABRIELLE: Left?

SOLANGE: I mean you or Paul: who left who?

GABRIELLE: I did.

SOLANGE: What is it they say? "A sin confessed is half redressed?"

GABRIELLE: I didn't need to confess, because I never saw it as a sin. I just wanted to meet the wife . . .

SOLANGE: . . .that he was cheating on. Anyway, I know he would be much happier with someone like you.

GABRIELLE: What a terrible way to think! How could you get to this point?

SOLANGE: What point?

GABRIELLE: To be so indifferent.

SOLANGE: We have an agreement. A lot of couples live this way. According to some kind of an agreement. In the past, couples got together to have children; they divided up the chores and put up with anything out of a sense of duty. Now that we've started looking for love everything is more complicated. People who don't find love make do. Make arrangements. They come to an agreement. You're courageous, to keep looking . . .

GABRIELLE: Courageous. Lacking courage kills people. I had a picture in my head, a picture of you based on what Paul told me about you.

47

SOLANGE: Paul never bothered to take the time to . . . Anyway, who is Paul, really? He's a mystery to me. Basically, he's pretty superficial, don't you think? You who know him so well?

GABRIELLE: I thought you knew everything, understood everything. That you were a model of fairness, understanding, of courage, since you mention it, but . . . Anyway, we're talking about Paul . . . Because he's the reason that I dragged myself over here, that I was willing to take the risk of being criticized. It's wrong to think that Paul deserves your disdain. It's wrong. Paul is someone who hides behind a lot of screens. His tears are very private. He's inside himself. When he cries, maybe you hear him and maybe you don't. He runs off to hide in his inner prison and you can't hear him. He's fallen into a deep pit, into a vacuum, but you're the one responsible for it because you didn't want to get close to him. You're afraid of him. And deep down he really does love you, but he loves you in his own way, and he expressed it awkwardly. What he always wanted . . . needed . . . was for you to make sense of everything, but instead you kept sending him back to a reflection, to this image you've created of him. And I acted the same way, because I just projected back this image I had of him as a seducer, a superficial male. I don't really have much courage. I don't have enough to . . .

SOLANGE: You're trying to save the world, aren't you?

GABRIELLE: No, I don't want to save the world.

SOLANGE: Listen. There are people who will be condemned, damned. There always have been and always will be.

GABRIELLE: That's a horrible thing to say. It's like all of a sudden the body must be made to pay, the heart has to atone for its sins. You're too hard on me. You're hurting but you don't want to admit it, so . . .

SOLANGE: Maybe I've decided that I'd be wasting my time trying to . . .

48

GABRIELLE: I've often thought that Paul is someone who is looking for something he's lost. A dream.

SOLANGE: Isn't that true of everyone? Doesn't everyone want to leave reality behind and lose himself in a dream world?

GABRIELLE: Or maybe leave the nightmare behind and escape into reality.

SOLANGE: Sure, sure. Listen here. When I met Paul, I had spent most of my life lost in books. And one day, I raised my eyes from the page. Someone was looking at my body. Undressing me with his eyes. For the first time in my life I felt naked. I met him in a library. He was looking for a book on the history of money. He thought I was the librarian. I played along. He always said he looked at my legs for the first time when he was going down an aisle between two rows of books. Before that, no one had ever noticed my legs. They didn't exist until that day. But that didn't last long. He got busy with other things again and I went back to my books. In between times, we got married. We woke up in the same bed. Can you understand that?

GABRIELLE: It's too bad life isn't a series of first times.

SOLANGE: The first time is the only time that counts. All the pros and cons can be weighed right there. Whatever you see at that moment, everything you feel, just gets more so as time goes on.

GABRIELLE: I meant that the world should be new. Constantly new. We should figure out some way of making everything new without giving up anyone or anything.

SOLANGE: It's only the body that needs novelty. It gets bored and ends up dragging down the rest. But for you, the body is something else. Isn't that right?

GABRIELLE: The body is what I found first. When I was very young, I felt abandoned. I wanted someone to take me in his arms, to warm me up, to . . . love me. I wanted to live inside my body. I wanted someone to fill up all that emptiness. But the problem is . . . the vacuum . . . my emptiness . . . it just got bigger and bigger.

10
THE SERMON ON SURVIVAL

I wanted to reign over your silence
I had so many things that I wanted to say
And while I was waiting the thread of my thoughts
 unravelled
And I was living in another era, in another world
I was screaming to myself
I was screaming more and more quietly

SOLANGE *[Speaking to a class]:* I have marked your assign-
ments. You can come and pick them up at the end of class.
As usual, I found the same problems. A lack of research, a
lack of organization. Enormous difficulties in writing
properly. At this level, there are errors that cannot be for-
given. Slang. Spelling: I won't even go into that again. In
some cases, I gave up correcting the mistakes; there were
so many of them. Horribly awkward sentences. Hand-
writing that was illegible. I had to guess what some of you
were thinking because I certainly couldn't read it.

As far as History goes . . . History, not what you ate
this morning . . . The subject of History . . . I don't know
where to begin. We can all read a book and transcribe
what we read. What I'm asking you to do, in this class, is
to develop some kind of linear thought, to be original, to
have ideas, you know, opinions about things. Not just to
copy what you read. Anyway, when you read my com-
ments you might notice how discouraged I'm getting. But
I'm not going to tell you how to live your lives. You'll figure it out. *[She picks up her lecture notes.]*

In our last class, we were talking about the Expulsion
of the Acadians, an event which, you remember, took

place in the middle of the eighteenth century and which stands as the most significant event in Acadian history, as a turning point in the evolution of the Acadian people. We could spend the entire course talking about the importance of this event and still not do it justice, but since we only have forty-five hours together, I'll try to be brief.

Most of the popular and mythical ideas that have prevailed about this tragic episode were passed on to us by the American poet Henry Wadsworth Longfellow, in his poem "Evangeline." Acadian history, seen from the point of view of the poem's heroine, Evangeline, evokes the great classical myths: Ulysses, the search for the Holy Grail . . . *[She realizes her audience is completely lost.]* The Grail is a legend about King Arthur's knights, who search for the goblet with which Christ first initiated the sacrament of the Eucharist; this is what he drank from when he said . . . you'll remember this from Communion: "This is My blood." Since it's such an important relic, a relic which is . . . well, let's say it's a powerful symbol in our imagination, and is probably connected to ancient magical rituals, the ancient idea of magic . . . but let's not go into that. The Grail is the cup from which Christ was supposed to have drunk. And Sir Galahad is the one who was to return it to the court of King Arthur because, it was said, he had a pure heart. What is a pure heart? We had better not get into that either.

So . . . um . . . Oh yes! Evangeline, one of the victims of the Expulsion, was to marry Gabriel the night before this tragedy separated them, and she spent the rest of her life searching for him, in the United States especially, and particularly in Louisiana . . . Grail and Gabriel even sound alike, don't they? Her search ends with her discovery of Gabriel on his death bed in a hospital where she is caring for the sick because, when she despaired of ever finding him again, she decided to become a nun. *[She looks at two or three students, who are laughing.]* You find that comical, do you? Obviously, the story is hardly a tribute to feminist thinking. It is a love story. They exist, you know; or maybe we should say they used to exist. So what do you think about these questions, you two down there? Since the beginning of the class you seem to have found a lot to laugh about. I was wondering if you would care to discuss love, your viewpoint on love, or just love in general. Do you think love has managed to survive feminism? Or is love something men invented and imposed on women? Go ahead. No need to be shy, we're all friends here. No comment? Fine . . .

11
INTELLIGENCE AS AN ESCAPE SYSTEM

*Through our reasoning, we finally conclude that the
        world is a plot, an error, an offence.
One day, we all finally meet someone
        who takes us by the hand.
When that person touches you, the world begins to exist.
I saw you passing in the night;
your heart was purity itself.
The complex resonance of my hollow emptiness.*

PAUL: It's pretty impressive that she came so far out.

SOLANGE: Who?

PAUL: Céline Dion.

SOLANGE: Do you mean to say we live in the boonies?

PAUL: She's an international star. The kind you see on the
    Tonight Show. And when you get to be on the Tonight
    Show, it's because you have a pretty powerful machine
    behind you. There's money backing you . . .

SOLANGE: Did it ever occur to you that she might have tal-
    ent?

PAUL: You certainly need to have some capital to get you start-
    ed on your way. It's like everything else . . .

SOLANGE: Oh my God! You see that guy down there? The
    one in gray and black . . .

PAUL: The tall one?

SOLANGE: Yeah. Change places with me. I don't want him to
    see me here.

PAUL: So you're ashamed to be seen with me, are you? What's
    with you?

SOLANGE: I guess I'm not myself.

PAUL: Who is this guy?

53

SOLANGE: Someone that I met the other day and I keep running into, in the oddest places. I get the feeling he's following me. I don't mean that he's hiding in a car with binoculars or taking pictures with a zoom lens, or anything like that, but he seems to show up everywhere I go.

PAUL: Mmm. Interesting. I think he's headed over here.

SOLANGE: Oh, no. Let's go. *[Thomas meets them on the way.]*

THOMAS *[To Paul]:* Do you have a light? I lost my lighter . . . Solange? What a coincidence!

SOLANGE: It seems we were destined to meet in public places.

THOMAS: Yes! Last time was at the mall.

SOLANGE: Well, it was good seeing you. *[To Paul.]* I'd better get back. I think it's going to start soon.

PAUL: No, no. We've got a good ten minutes yet. I think I'll go get a Pepsi.

THOMAS: Are you enjoying the show?

PAUL: It's well done. You can tell she's a pro. What do you think?

THOMAS: I liked her better when she sang "The Dove . . ."

SOLANGE *[Incredulous]:* The theme song for the Pope's visit?

PAUL: She's come a long way since then.

THOMAS: Yes, but back then she was a very young woman, sort of innocent and natural. She had such a strong voice. You could tell she was sure of herself already, but so pure. Yes, she certainly has changed a lot since.

PAUL: Don't we all?

THOMAS: So how is your research on the Expulsion coming along? Are you getting through it?

SOLANGE: Oh, yes, I'm getting along just fine. It's a lot of work, but I'll get it done. I've just started reading a book of eighteenth-century psalms that I found. There are some that are really beautiful. It would be tempting to assume that those were the ones the Acadians sang at the time, but I'd better do some more serious research before I draw any conclusions.

THOMAS: They aren't all like the Song of Songs.

SOLANGE [A little embarrassed]: No, I don't see much similarity. I don't think they were very interested in The Song of Solomon.

PAUL: I'd better leave this discussion to you scholars. I'm going to get something to drink. Do you want anything?

SOLANGE: We can change the subject if you're bored, Paul.

PAUL: No, no. I just felt like a coffee. Go ahead and talk; I'll be back soon. [Exits.]

THOMAS: Is that your husband?

SOLANGE: Yes. Paul. When he gets back, I'll introduce you officially.

THOMAS: I've been thinking about you a lot since our last conversation.

SOLANGE: So have I.

THOMAS: Yet it seemed like such an ordinary conversation at the time. I only remember that we laughed. That's something that doesn't happen to me often. I like your laugh. I hear your laughter in my head for no apparent reason. It's like an obsession with me.

SOLANGE: Have you noticed that fewer and fewer people smoke? Last time there were twice as many of us freezing outside . . .

THOMAS: You don't want to talk about the things that remind me of you.

SOLANGE: I don't want to put a name to what's happening. I don't like to say it out loud. And I also don't want to say it because, as soon as we call it by its name, it will really exist.

THOMAS: And you're afraid of it.

SOLANGE: I'm afraid for you.

THOMAS: You shouldn't be afraid for other people. You should never be afraid to tell people how important they are to you, what a miracle it is that they are here on earth with you. Sharing your space and time. Maybe it's yourself you're afraid of.

SOLANGE: Or maybe I'm just not the kind of person who's good at talking about that sort of thing. I'm not good at these . . . situations.

THOMAS: How do you know?

SOLANGE: I got my ideas about life from books. You must know all about that, too.

THOMAS: It took a lot of courage to talk to you about all of this, I must admit. This is the first time that something like this has ever happened to me. Let me tell you, sometimes I even think that the devil is tempting me, testing my flesh. But as soon as I decide to stop seeing you once and for all, then fate puts you in my path once again. And each time you are more attractive, more seductive than before.

SOLANGE: The devil can take many forms, why shouldn't he appear as me? Is that what you mean? The devil. The very word seems to come out of some earlier era.

THOMAS: But has anything really changed so much since then?

SOLANGE: We have more knowledge now. It's as simple as that. We are more intelligent than people used to be. More civilized.

THOMAS: That hasn't helped us resolve the problem of evil.

SOLANGE: What is evil?

THOMAS: What is truth?

SOLANGE: The famous reply of Pontius Pilate.

THOMAS: I can't help it. You ask questions that no man can answer.

SOLANGE: No woman, either, I presume.

THOMAS: No woman. All my life I've behaved as though women were abstract ideas.

SOLANGE: And yet you hear their sins when they confess. Their words must not seem so abstract at confession.

THOMAS: Confession is a sacrament by which God soothes suffering and evil. There's nothing voyeuristic about hearing confessions. In the end, the way people list their sins, their account book of evil deeds, it just becomes tedious. There's a world of difference between word and deed.

SOLANGE: That sounds like a new area of research someone should do.

THOMAS: Don't change the subject.

SOLANGE: I hid in my books to get away from this kind of discussion. I feel extremely uneasy when someone brings the idea of the body back into the discussion.

THOMAS: I'm concerned less with your body than with the quality of your mind, the depth of our conversations when we speak, the ideas that you handle so . . .

SOLANGE: If you only knew how little I've learned. At least from my own point of view. My confidence is just there to cover up a vacuum. Emptiness. I don't feel very seductive.

THOMAS: How can you ignore the body when you talk about love?

SOLANGE: What is love?

THOMAS: What is truth?

SOLANGE: I dreamed about you the other night.

THOMAS: I dream about you all day, all night, all the time. You pop into my head; you come back to me on the most unpredictable occasions. And when I see you . . .

SOLANGE: I want to talk about something else.

THOMAS: What was I doing, in your dream?

SOLANGE: We were touring a temple. The group moved on and we stayed behind, together. Suddenly, I noticed that there was a crack in the wall. You leaned up against the wall and a door opened. It was a secret passageway that led to an idol. Its eyes were red and bright like two enormous rubies. I was afraid, all of a sudden, that someone would come and close the door on us and I turned around to see . . . [Paul returns.]

PAUL: So do you feel like going in for the rest of the show? I noticed there was an empty seat next to Solange, if you're interested.

THOMAS: Actually, I left my coat on the seat I was in.

PAUL: It will only take you a minute to go back and get it. That way you could continue your conversation.

SOLANGE: Paul, let him sit where he likes. Why are you being so insistent?

PAUL: No reason. I just thought that since you two knew each other . . .

THOMAS: Thank you, but I'd rather sit alone. I'm not even sure that I'll be staying until the end.

SOLANGE: Oh, yes, I forgot. Thomas, I'd like you to meet Paul, my husband.

12
ESCAPE AS A SURVIVAL SYSTEM

At this very instant, someone is coming into the world. At this very instant, a love is dying out, someone has lost a set of keys, someone is being kissed for the very first time. At this very instant someone has picked up a child, someone has lit a cigarette, someone is in the process of giving up the ghost, someone has gotten lost in the forest, someone is waiting for someone.

> *[In the waiting room of a hospital. Gabrielle is sitting, alone, reading a magazine. Thomas enters, looks around, notices her, and heads towards her.]*

THOMAS: Hello, Gabrielle. Are you waiting for someone?

GABRIELLE: Thomas?

THOMAS: No, I'm not a vision. Not a hologram, either.

GABRIELLE: I seem to run into you everywhere these days.

THOMAS: Especially here.

GABRIELLE: Other places, too.

THOMAS: What are you doing in the waiting room? You're not sick, I hope.

GABRIELLE: No, I told someone to meet me here.

THOMAS: Really? At this hour? In a waiting room?

GABRIELLE: Yes. And he's late, I see. How is Martin doing?

THOMAS: Yesterday, when I went to see him, he seemed pretty weak. Anyone else who had gone through what he had would be dead by now. Those people must have such strength!

GABRIELLE: He must appreciate your visits. For people like him, the priest is someone who matters. I mean, it helps them get through hard times.

THOMAS: These days, I'm the one who needs his help.

GABRIELLE: Are you leaving the priesthood?

THOMAS: You must be kidding!

GABRIELLE: Have you got a girlfriend? The other day, I saw you with a woman. I caught you! I caught you!

THOMAS: Well. Visiting hours have started.

GABRIELLE: Thomas, I was only kidding. I didn't mean anything by it. You can talk to me about what's bothering you, if you like, and I'll listen. Really. I'm sorry.

THOMAS: No, it really is visiting hours, Gabrielle, and I have to get going.

GABRIELLE: Okay. Come and say bye before you go.

THOMAS: We'll see.

GABRIELLE: Thomas, that's enough. Really. Thomas . . . [Thomas goes upstairs. Gabrielle watches him go and stays where she is for a few minutes. She picks up a magazine, looks at her watch. For thirty seconds, at least, she sits there, alone with hospital noises. Paul arrives.]

PAUL: Some place to meet someone! What were you thinking?

GABRIELLE: You said you needed to see me. You told me to pick the place. I chose this one.

PAUL: Yeah, but still. This place . . . And at two in the afternoon, in the middle of visiting hours.

GABRIELLE: Last time we met, it was in a tavern. You think that was any better?

PAUL: No one would run into us in a . . .

GABRIELLE: Exactly. That's why I decided I wanted to talk to you here, Paul. I'm tired of hiding out in dark corners and alleyways. I want to live in daylight, now. Live. In the middle of the day. Out in the sun.

PAUL: But it was to protect us . . .

GABRIELLE: Protect us from what?

PAUL: Listen, I didn't come here to talk about the weather.

GABRIELLE: So what's so important? On the phone it sounded like a matter of life and death.

Paul: Well, it's about us. What's going to happen to us? It is a matter of life and death, you're right. It's a matter of life and death.

GABRIELLE: Too late. It's already happened. Now we have to let time take its . . .

PAUL: I don't believe you, Gabrielle. I don't believe this . . .

GABRIELLE: Shh. Quiet down.

PAUL: You're the one who wanted to meet in this hole . . .

GABRIELLE: It's called a hospital.

PAUL: Well, in my opinion, a hospital is a . . .

GABRIELLE: What? Say it.

PAUL: It's a slaughterhouse. Every time I come here, it's to see someone who's dying. As far as I'm concerned, it's not a very good place to talk about a relationship that's alive.

GABRIELLE: Relationships die too. Only love . . .

PAUL: Maybe that's why you wanted to meet me here. Because you want to kill our relationship. You want to put it out of its misery . . .

GABRIELLE: Misery. Interesting choice of words. Yes, I'd go as far as to say it was stillborn.

PAUL: Well, you didn't take long to recover.

GABRIELLE: I need something free and easy for now. Something to help me heal. I don't have many expectations right now.

PAUL: You're not as insensitive as you seem. It must do something to you . . .

GABRIELLE: If you have something you want to tell me . . . I only have half an hour. I worked things out with a friend and I have to get back in fifteen minutes, no matter what. If you had got here on time . . .

PAUL: I've done everything to try to get you out of my life. I hate myself for being so weak, so easy to manipulate. I need you. I've never said that to anyone before, and I hate being so dependent. But you're like a drug . . . I have to do something, go into detox or therapy or something.

GABRIELLE: We never even talked about love, you know.

PAUL: I know. I realized that, afterwards.

61

GABRIELLE: Too little, too late.

PAUL: You never realize how important people are to you. The people in your life who really matter.

GABRIELLE: You don't have to tell me that.

PAUL: Who should I be telling? Solange?

GABRIELLE: Hire someone. Start a journal. Go see a priest, or talk to Solange. But as long as you're talking to me, you're just going to hurt yourself more. I'm not the right person to talk to. Not anymore.

PAUL: You are the right person. It's because of you that all this happened.

GABRIELLE: No. I'm going to put an end to this once and for all. I've already paid my dues. No one is going to make me feel like I still owe them. I've decided that my life is my own. My mother spent years trying to make me feel like a whore because I discovered I had a body and thought she should have had one. And because she didn't, she would have preferred that I didn't either. Do you get it, Paul? You have no right to hold me responsible. You made free choices, full well knowing. You consented. Get that into your head.

PAUL: Not so loud.

GABRIELLE: Have you got that through your head, now?

PAUL: Why don't you return my calls?

GABRIELLE: Because I'm not home much.

PAUL: Don't tell me you're still dating that guy.

GABRIELLE: I'm not home much.

PAUL: Are you doing all this on purpose? If I had known things would turn out this badly, I would have turned and run away the first night we met.

GABRIELLE: Paul, I've already said that I want us to be friends. But the way you're acting I'd be surprised if that happens any time soon.

PAUL: What do you expect? I can't help how I feel.

GABRIELLE: You know what I think you're having a hard time with? We don't sleep together anymore. And so you act like a child who throws a tantrum because he thinks that's the way to get back what someone took away from him.

PAUL: These things change . . .

GABRIELLE: If I were a thing, maybe. But . . .

PAUL: I don't know what else to say.

GABRIELLE: Maybe that's the best idea. Don't say anything.

PAUL: What a life!

GABRIELLE: Maybe a large dose of silence will help you get over it. Maybe you'll see your way clear. It isn't easy for me, either, you know.

PAUL: Do you want to talk about it?

GABRIELLE: No, it would be too easy for you to put me in a vulnerable position.

PAUL: I can see you really trust me.

GABRIELLE: I waited too long. When you wait for something too long, it comes out all wrong. Anyway, there's no school to teach you these things. The school of life . . . And to think that there are people who ruin their lives, and I was so determined not to be someone like that. I have to live with myself. But others seem to have taken away everything that mattered. I was like a fire sale. A garage sale. You must have come along at the wrong time. At the time I decided to clear everything out.

PAUL: And you dumped me out with the rest of the trash.

GABRIELLE: You know, you don't make it easy. Did you ever think that maybe there were other people who have lives, souls, hearts, too, Paul? And that's probably all they have that really belongs to them.

PAUL: Everyone knows that.

GABRIELLE: There's a world of difference between knowing something and believing it.

PAUL: Shall I come by for you after work?

GABRIELLE: You've certainly mastered the art of avoidance. Why . . . *[Thomas enters. He looks troubled.]*

THOMAS: Hello, Paul.

GABRIELLE: Is it Martin?

THOMAS: An hour ago, at the most. I stayed with the family for a while. I think they're relieved that it's over. Now they can give in to their grief. It will do them good to cry.

PAUL: Someone you knew well?

THOMAS: Someone I got to know well. Actually, what does that really mean? What does it mean to know someone?

13
THE ELEGANCE OF MUTUAL LIES

You will tell me that you didn't know and I will pretend not to know. You will tell me that the suffering has stopped and we will look, together, at the doorway. And when we awake we will pretend that we have dreamed it all. Just as we used to believe, blindly, that life was rich with promises.

SOLANGE: Could I offer you a Pernod? Kir? White wine?

THOMAS: A beer. I don't have very sophisticated tastes.

PAUL: I'll go and get one for you, Mister . . .

THOMAS: Thomas. No one calls me by my last name.

PAUL: I'm from the old school. I was raised to call everyone Mr. and Miss. Sorry . . .

SOLANGE: I find that a Pernod sits better on my stomach than a beer. Beer is so heavy . . .

GABRIELLE: Only people who have travelled in Europe really appreciate Pernod though.

THOMAS: But it's beer that quenches your thirst. I'm so thirsty I could . . . What's the expression for thirst? I could eat a horse: that's for hunger, but for thirst . . .

SOLANGE: There isn't one for thirst.

GABRIELLE: We don't talk about our thirst.

PAUL: Since these language questions go way over my head, I think I'll just go and serve the drinks.

SOLANGE: No, no, I'll go. I think I'd like to play hostess, for once.

PAUL: But if I stay here, the level of discussion is bound to drop considerably.

SOLANGE: You'll think of something. *[Exits.]*

PAUL: You know, I was a beer drinker, too, until I had enough money to buy Scotch.

THOMAS: It's not just money it takes, you have to develop a taste for it, appreciate it. It's like wine.

PAUL: Well, as far as that goes, we all drank wine at communion when we were children. It didn't help develop our taste.

THOMAS: Things have changed a lot in that respect.

GABRIELLE: I'm going to help Solange.

THOMAS: I didn't realize that Solange knew Gabrielle.

PAUL: Apparently they met during the student demonstrations, when they occupied the administration offices at the University. They ran into each other the other day. I didn't know anything about it until then.

THOMAS: The 1960s. Those were quite the times. So how's business?

PAUL: I suppose it's fine. But I'm not really a business man.

THOMAS: Well, you're a bank manager, and the banks are the only ones making money because that's where all the money is.

PAUL: I didn't realize you were interested in finance.

THOMAS: Goodness, no, I'm not. It's just an idea I heard on the radio the other day . . .

PAUL: Priests aren't what they used to be! After all, the Vatican is one of the biggest corporations in the world.

THOMAS: People aren't what they used to be either.

PAUL: Do you think they've really changed?

THOMAS: I'm sure you've seen children sitting in front of the TV or a video game. They seem to be hypnotized. They look possessed, or like they're in some kind of mystical trance. Maybe the world is under a hypnotic spell and is waiting for some kind of saviour or exterminator. The only thing that can save us, or at least give us the courage we need . . .

PAUL: Could you excuse me a moment? Someone is beckoning to me. I'll be right back.

SOLANGE: I see you've been abandoned. Here, take this. I'm afraid it warmed up a bit on the way. You know . . .

THOMAS: Solange, can I tell you something?

SOLANGE: Listen, I've already told you. I need to have some distance . . .

THOMAS: I know I shouldn't have come, but Gabrielle insisted. She really didn't want to come alone. I was the only one available and she didn't want to back out at the last minute. Your friendship . . .

SOLANGE: That's a pretty strong term. We hardly know each other.

THOMAS: I know, but she wants things to work out between you.

SOLANGE: She told you what happened?

THOMAS: No, but I can guess. The other day, I saw her with Paul again, and since my sister has always been a little . . .

SOLANGE: Loose. To put it mildly.

THOMAS: How did you take it? Finding out about it?

SOLANGE: I always knew about it. Not about your sister, in particular, but in a general sense. Maybe men annoy me.

THOMAS: That's too bad. You have every charm you need to attract them.

SOLANGE: Charm? I don't know. But not the will. They taught us all about the will in school, and it served me well there. But I seemed to falter in life. In real life.

THOMAS: Real life. As though there is some other kind that is an illusion.

SOLANGE: Native Americans believed that the world was an illusion, and that life was a dream.

THOMAS: It's too bad they didn't convert us.

SOLANGE: That's a surprising statement, coming from you.

THOMAS: Christ said: "Not every one that saith unto me, Lord, Lord, shall enter into the Kingdom of heaven; but he that doeth the will of my Father . . ." *[The light on Solange and Thomas fades, and moves to Paul and Gabrielle.]*

GABRIELLE: You know the painting ou wanted to buy? You're right, it would look good on that wall over there.

PAUL: You met Solange, didn't you?

GABRIELLE: I was tired of hearing you talk about her like she was some kind of monster. I wanted to see what kind of a monster she was. I wanted to peek into her cave, even if it meant being eaten alive.

PAUL: You weren't running much of a risk, considering I had never told her anything about us.

GABRIELLE: And that's exactly why I told her everything.

PAUL: Why did you do that? How could you?

GABRIELLE: Did I really have any choice?

PAUL: What?

GABRIELLE: I have to get on with my life, Paul. When your suffering is over, you will have forgotten me. But I'm going to be left with all those memories and I have to make some kind of sense out of them. It's not your problem. I know you'll work something out for yourself, but I have to make peace with myself, to forgive myself before I'm through.

PAUL: What I see going on here . . . You want me to tell you? Do you want me to tell you what I see going on here? What I see is someone out for revenge, being cruel out of sheer selfishness, because despite all your principles, nothing good will come out of all this.

GABRIELLE: I don't care if anything good comes out of it. Or anything at all, for that matter. Nothing will really change, anyway, because Solange has given up too. Solange, in fact, is still wondering what her life might have been. What good will come of that?

PAUL: I don't know. Why don't you ask your new friend? Between friends, you can confide in each other. No secrets. I really hate myself. I hate myself for having been so naïve.

GABRIELLE: I want to go, Paul. I'm really feeling uneasy here. And if I have too much to drink, things might get ugly, and right at this moment that doesn't seem like such a bad thing. So to keep things in order . . . Watch me when I walk out the door. It's the last time you'll ever see me. Because after that I'm going to turn out the lights and we'll all be in the dark. Including me. That's what scares me. People like me would do anything to not be left alone. They'd even give their bodies to strangers. Or pretend to.

PAUL: I didn't mean to say those things. I was talking without thinking.

GABRIELLE: It doesn't matter. We'll get over it. Life goes on. It has to go on. It doesn't have any other choice. *[Lights focus on Solange and Thomas.]*

SOLANGE: I know that one day, turning the corner somewhere, I'm going to come across a woman who is me, the carnal envelope of my self. I'll reconnect with my body and it will be like a skin graft, a heart transplant, a landing in outer space . . .

THOMAS: Once, when I was a child, someone gave me a plastic model of the human body as a Christmas present. All of the pieces were transparent. There were pots of paint that came with it, and a chart that told you what colour to paint each part. But I decided I liked it better with transparent body parts. I had the feeling that that was the way my own body was. Transparent.

SOLANGE: We seem to be suffering from the same problem.

THOMAS: I was thinking: maybe we could help each other heal.

SOLANGE: Do you believe in miracles?

THOMAS: The ones you can make happen, yes. But it is not enough to know how or to be able to. You also have to want to and . . .

GABRIELLE: Thomas, I want to go home. You can stay here if you like; I'll take a taxi.

THOMAS: No, I want to go home too. I have a funeral tomorrow . . .

GABRIELLE: You too?

THOMAS: What do you mean, you too?

PAUL: So . . . what's everyone drinking?

THOMAS: Nothing more for me. My glass is still full. Full and warm . . .

PAUL: Can I get you a cold one?

SOLANGE: Paul. Gabrielle wants to go home. I don't think she's feeling well.

PAUL: No, no. It'll pass. It's nothing a good Scotch can't fix. Cures what ails you. *[Gabrielle begins to move towards the door.]*

SOLANGE: Paul, stop being foolish. You can see that she's . . .

THOMAS: Thanks for the wonderful evening. It's been very pleasant, and I hope it will continue being so for many hours yet. Anyway, I wasn't planning on staying as long as I did. As I said, I have a sermon to prepare and . . .

PAUL: The party has barely started.

THOMAS: I'd better go with her. *[Exits.]*

PAUL: Well, I guess it's true what they say. You can't please everyone. You're the one who wanted to invite them.

SOLANGE: I invited Gabrielle. She's the one who decided to bring along her brother.

PAUL: When did you meet Gabrielle?

SOLANGE: Don't try to play innocent, Paul. That's probably the first question you asked during that little conversation you just had with her. I'm sure you know the answer.

PAUL: It's over between us.

SOLANGE: Between you and me or between you and her?

PAUL: Mmm . . .

SOLANGE: I've decided that I'm leaving, Paul.

PAUL: Not because of this little incident, I hope.

SOLANGE: I haven't really been with you for some time now.

PAUL: What's with you all, anyway?

SOLANGE: It's time to take action. Do something.

PAUL: Gabrielle put these ideas into your head, didn't she?

SOLANGE: My head is full of ideas, Paul. The problem is that they usually just sit there in my head. Up until now, I've always been reasonable.

PAUL: There's nothing wrong with that. You're acting like there's something evil about being sensible.

SOLANGE: What is evil?

PAUL: Evil is making a fool out of somebody.

SOLANGE: That's an interesting moral principle.

PAUL: We have a houseful of people. You certainly have great timing.

SOLANGE: Why don't we tell them what's going on? That way, at least, twenty people will get the same version. What do you think?

PAUL: Separating is out of style, haven't you heard? These days, people mate for life. They get more married as time goes by.

SOLANGE: Maybe we're aging against the passage of time.

PAUL: This whole thing is like a nightmare.

SOLANGE: Maybe it's the beginning of a new dream.

PAUL: Either way, we're bound to wake up one day or another.

14
THE PARTISANS OF TIME

I will take the earth in my hands and fill the pockets of my coat with it, the way we did when we walked in the same tracks, to remember the winter when the earth was buried under the snow, to say that time is only a handful of sand that leaks out of coat pockets.

THOMAS: We are gathered here, in the company of believers, to pray together and to bid a last farewell to our brother Martin, who has left us for a place where he will find peace and salvation. For his family, naturally, these are trying times. To his children, his grandchildren and his great grandchildren, to the whole family, I would like to speak on behalf of the community here in conveying our sympathies and in telling you that our hearts are with you in your suffering. Those of us who are left here are crying, but he is in a state of joy, not because he has left us — I know he would have wanted to be with us this morning — but because now he has arrived in a safe haven.

Even if our brother Martin suffered in the last while, even if we can believe that, in his case, death has delivered him from his pain, someone said to me a few minutes ago in the funeral parlour that he had heart problems he hid from his family, so that he would not burden them, or worry them, for more than anything else, he wanted those he loved to be happy. Even if he took risks with his health.

Even if our brother suffered, he always wanted his suffering to bring him closer to the Lord. A few days before his death, he told me that his pain helped him to understand the sacrifice that the Lord made for our sins, and he thus felt closer and closer to God in his last days. He wanted, also, to join his beloved wife and the dear departed family members who awaited him in heaven, and he was comforted by the certainty that they would all find themselves together once more at the table of the Lord. This faith and trust in the afterlife, at the time when we finally feel weak and know that we are leaving this world; this faith and trust, at the time we are leaving this life and all those who are close to us on earth, should be a lesson to us all. His example should help us to have hope and to have faith that we will finally see the face of God and enter into the light of His love.

Of course, death is always a time of great sorrow. It's a time that leaves scars and that sometimes opens old wounds. We remember all the happy occasions and all the difficult moments we shared with the deceased and we try to make peace with ourselves. We wish we could revise those moments when we should have tempered our words or our deeds, when we should have done or said something a little differently. There are words that should never have been spoken and that will remain with us like awful silences deep inside of us. That's why it is important, at a time like this, to make our peace with the deceased. Important for us, also, for those of us left behind, for this community of the living, to learn how to speak with an open heart instead of letting things build up. We need to learn to live without being able to speak to the only person who should hear what we have to say, that is, the dearly departed.

As you know, we Acadians are often blamed for this habit. It is true that we frequently tend to be silent rather than to speak. This silence, in the long run, has become a weight that burdens us; we carry it on our shoulders so long that it becomes almost unbearable. And I am not referring only to the trouble we have saying things that may make us seem unpleasant or damage our favourable reputations. We must also learn not to be afraid to say to people we care about how happy we are that they are there, how happy we are that they are alive, and that it is because of them that our lives are more enjoyable. To tell them how easy it is, because of their presence in our lives, to give ourselves over to our faith and to continue our journey towards the house of the Lord.

I have no doubt that our brother Martin left us, a few days ago, to enter into that house. And that is the place where he will await us. Those who knew him, especially his family, will tell you how conscientious a father and how devoted a husband he was. Naturally, some will say that "in our day, that was how life was, that was how things were done" and will add, perhaps, that "those people didn't know any better." It is true that they did not have television, computers, Nintendo games or four-lane highways. They did not have free love or holidays in Florida. They did not know about cellular phones, compact discs, VCRs. They did not have unemployment insurance, social assistance, or government subsidies. They lived in an era where everyone was poor and honest, and they believed that their misery would help them to grow. Sad to say, today we almost wish we could go back in time to rediscover the simple pleasures they found in life. That is why we might say today that a whole world is following Martin into the ground.

It is true that we might be tempted to conclude, when we look at all of this from a distance, when we think about what they did not have, that these people didn't know anything about modern life. They were not influenced by ideas that came from outside of their community. Most of them could not read. However, they lived in harmony with nature and with the laws of the universe. Hope dictated their actions; they knew how to help each other and knew that they would, in return, be admitted into their Father's mansion. Their faith enabled them to build a whole world without ever questioning or wondering what was the point of it all, what good could come of all this. Love and sharing kept them close to each other, for it is through our love that we manage to change our world.

The Lord is my Shepherd, I shall not want. So often we hear how difficult it is to walk in the footsteps of the Lord, often we let ourselves fall into the belief that life is too hard for us, that it burdens us intolerably, that our obligations outnumber our moments of grace, our happiness and our communion with people around us. And yet, God made this world for us. He made it for us to find a reason to live in it. For us to work together to remake it in His image, so that we might complete the world He started in beauty and joy.

Printed in April 2006
at Gauvin Press, Gatineau, Québec